THINKING ON THESE THINGS

A BIBLE STUDY FROM
PHILIPPIANS 4:8

Ruth Ann Larkly

THINKING ON THESE THINGS

Dedication

When I first began to study Philippians 4:7-8, I prayed about how I could share these biblical truths with others. I felt led to make several Facebook live videos on my "Happy as a Larkly" ministry page (called "Larkly Ladies Bible Studies" back then). Feeling nervous, I made an introductory video about my troubles with swallowing and the battle in my mind. I confidently announced (gulp!) I would go live on "Mindful Monday" and "Follow-up Friday" with video lessons from Philippians 4:7-8.

For all of you who messaged, called, responded, reacted, shared, watched, or liked my videos—I dedicate this book to you. I felt your comfort instead of condemnation. Sensing God's grace, I began to heal. I watched in awe as He took a trial, in which I felt defeated, to be used for His glory.

You told me I was a blessing to you, but here is the honest truth—you were the biggest blessing to me. God used you, my sisters in Christ, to be a part of my mental health journey. I will always be thankful for you being there for me during that hard season of my life. Hugs and love to you all!

Table of Contents

Acknowledgements

I would like to thank my husband, Tim. Many times, people ask me questions about self-publishing and getting my studies into book form. I have an easy answer: "It's Tim. He does everything—from communicating with the publishing company, to page layouts and formatting. He even designs the front and back cover."

I also know Tim does more than that. His support and encouragement with my writing has strengthened me to not quit and keep going. He has encouraged me to take time to write and attend a monthly writer's club. Many times he would arrange or re-arrange his schedule to help with the family. He listened when I felt down, or rejoiced when I experienced a breakthrough.

Tim, this is the fifth Bible study you have done for me. I believe it is the best one yet. I know how much time you have sacrificed to make this happen. Thank you from the bottom of my heart. I love you!

I would like to thank my friend Christie Shellenberger. Thank you for proofreading these chapters. I know when you agreed to do so, you had many other commitments going at the same time. You undertook this task with dedication and enthusiasm. Many, many times you heard me share the ebbs and flows of this study. Thank you for always listening, encouraging, and cheering me on!

I would like to thank all my friends from my writing group called Word Weavers in Cottonwood, Arizona. You have read through every chapter of this study and offered helpful and constructive feedback. Due to my family's ministry move to southern Arizona, I miss all of you. May God bless you as you have been a blessing to me!

Preface:
Why I Wrote this
Bible Study from Philippians 4:8

In September at the age of 40, I began to feel pain when swallowing my food. It concerned me because I had a history of health issues with my stomach and throat: my gallbladder had been taken out at 16, I had GERD and a weak esophagus by 18, and stomach and bile issues up to age 25. I decided to get serious about my health and lost 60 pounds in two years. More importantly, I felt my body beginning to heal.

I'm sharing with you these health issues for you to see why I began to freak out when I couldn't swallow. Every bite and sip I took hurt, but something even more painful took place—a battle in my mind. It involved enemies, lies, and weapons. I allowed myself to think, "I must have throat cancer." The doctor had warned me about that when I was 18.

Next, I did the WORST possible thing. I googled "not able to swallow." What do you think popped up? Throat cancer. Oh sure, other possibilities also popped up, but I fixated my mind on the worst case scenario. I'm sad to say I began to believe and think false lies from the devil during this time.

I took immediate physical action. (Oh, how I wish I took more spiritual action!) I changed my diet to see if I had food allergies, saw a gastroenterologist, and made an appointment for a scope test. During this time, I maintained my Bible reading and prayer time every morning. I always attended church (okay, my husband's a preacher so this wasn't even an option!). I wrote in my prayer journal and listened to spiritually uplifting music. I had my good days, and then I had my bad.

The first week of November I flew to South Dakota to visit a dear friend of mine. On Sunday morning, I remember praying and asking the

9

Lord to please give me something, anything, to help me. In Sunday school, the lesson was a study on the names of God. When I heard about the Lord as "Adonai," I teared up hearing about the Master's love and care for His servants.

For the main worship service, because the pastor had some health issues, a layman got up to speak. He apologized for not being a preacher and said he just wanted to read some verses and talk about them. He read Philippians 4:7-8, and I followed along. When I read, "…whatsoever things are of a good report" my mind stopped. WAIT, what? The phrase leaped off my Bible page and into my heart.

In that moment, I believed God wanted me to think a good report for my upcoming scope test. I believed He didn't want me to think on things of doom and gloom. Instead, to think on things true, honest, just, pure, lovely, a good report, virtuous, and praiseworthy.

I quietly cried right there on the pew, and I went forward to pray at the altar during the invitation time. My heart felt lighter than ever. From that moment, did I only think on things from Philippians 4:8? No, but it became a start.

A few weeks later my husband Tim preached at another church. On a back table I found a magnet that said: "Places to Park your Mind." It had a picture of a van in a parking lot and the list of things from Philippians 4:8. I took it home, stuck it on my fridge, and committed the verse to memory. (Hey, it's harder than you think!)

The morning of my scope test, the Holy Spirit comforted me and gave me such peace through His Word. After my test, I heard the good report that my throat looked great! The gastroenterologist explained to me I couldn't swallow because my stomach had gone up into my esophagus. Oh, the relief to not have throat cancer.

For the next three weeks I took the prescribed medicine by the doctor to help my stomach go down. It never helped, and I quit taking it. That's when Tim had the idea our family chiropractor might be able to help.

When the chiropractor began to ask me some questions, a light bulb turned on in my head. In September, my ribs had begun to ache after attending a ladies' retreat. When I had been playing inflatable basketball on an uneven dirt field, I had run with the ball, tripped over the bottom inflatable ring, and landed smack dab on my ribs. The wind got knocked out of me, and I missed the shot for my team. At the time, my ego hurt more than my ribs!

It took the chiropractor about 20 minutes to make the adjustments. He said my cartilage had separated from my ribs, causing my stomach to go up into my esophagus. As I left his office, he assured me I should be able to go home and eat with no problems.

I raced home to make and eat a toasted sandwich with all the fixings. Sure enough, I could swallow. Oh, happy moment! Throughout the day I kept eating and rejoicing. After three months, was it all finally over?

Later that night, different emotions swept over me: feelings of guilt, embarrassment, and sadness. Guilt because I allowed myself to be anxious and fearful, embarrassment because I hadn't handled my trial well, and sadness because of what I had allowed to enter and think on in my mind.

In January, two months later, I decided to do a personal Bible study of Philippians 4:7-8. Did you catch the word *personal*? Believe me, I certainly hadn't planned on sharing anything I went through or studied with anybody. If anything, I planned to keep my spiritual battle and nurse my wounds to myself.

But something happened inside me. A fire lit in my heart, a desire, to share with others those two powerful verses from Philippians 4:7-8. Though I am an internet introvert (and an in-person extrovert), I decided to make a Facebook live video on my Happy as a Larkly page (called "Larkly Ladies Bible Studies" back then).

Feeling nervous, I made an introductory video about my troubles with swallowing and the battle in my mind. I confidently announced (gulp!) I would go live on Mondays and Fridays with video lessons from Philippians 4:7-8.

Thank you to those of you who listened to me share the things that I had been learning. You will never know how much your words encouraged me and kept me going throughout the process. It both amazed and humbled me how God could use a trial I went through and felt defeated to be a help and an encouragement for others.

The devil loves it when we wallow in feelings of defeat, doesn't he? But guess what? I don't belong in his family. Defeat isn't in my name. I claim victory through my Lord Jesus Christ and peace from my Prince of Peace. I don't fight to win—I fight because I have already won.

As you fight on the battlefield of your mind, you can be assured to know that Philippians 4:7-8 equips, prepares, and strengthens you for your battles. These two verses reveal a secret to spiritual victory and success. They have changed my life, and it is my hope they will change yours as well. May the Lord use Philippians 4:7-8 to give you victory in your mind and life. —Happy Thinking on These Things!

Introduction

When I first began to study Philippians 4:8, I assumed I knew the meaning for the phrase *think on.* Philippians 4:8 says, "Finally, brethren, whatsoever things are true, whatsoever things are honest, whatsoever things are just, whatsoever things are pure, whatsoever things are lovely, whatsoever things are of good report; if there be any virtue, and if there be any praise, *think on these things*" (emphasis mine).

Doesn't the word *think* just mean to…well, think? Well, yes; for sure it does. However, this word *think* goes a little deeper. When the apostle Paul wrote it, he used the Greek word "logizomai," which means "to take inventory, account, number, reckon, or reason."[1] Paul relates our thinking process in our minds to taking an inventory or an account.

I know all about inventory lists. In my sophomore and junior year of college, I used to work at Burger King. I remember one job I hated—taking inventory of the frozen foods in the walk-in freezer. (Brrr. One time my shoes literally froze to the floor!) I knew I had an important job. How terrible if we ever ran out of onion rings, chicken strips, or French fries.

Taking inventory means you know what you have, what you need to have, what needs to be pitched, and what needs to be rotated or rearranged. It may involve a list with items, scribbles, notes, checks, and cross-off lines.

Just like you take a mindful account for your physical needs, how much more should you for your spiritual needs? From Philippians 4:8, you have an inventory list for your mind.

---

[1] Definition taken from *Strong's Greek Dictionary*. This study will reference original words and their meanings from both the *Strong's Hebrew* and *Strong's Greek Dictionary*.

☑ Things that are True

☑ Things that are Honest

☑ Things that are Just

☑ Things that are Pure

☑ Things that are Lovely

☑ Things of a Good Report

☑ Things of Virtue

☑ Things of Praise

We need to add these eight things in our minds. Each item on this inventory list will strengthen your mind and help you fight the battle in your mind. May God give you mental health and mental strength as you think on these things!

Chapter One

God's Peace

*Philippians 4:7: "And the **peace** of God, which passeth all understanding, shall keep your hearts and minds through Christ Jesus."*

Have you ever asked yourself, "How can I have peace in my mind?" That's the question I asked myself over and over while fighting the raging battle in mind. I would say to myself, "I just want peace in my mind."

I'm happy to tell you Philippians 4:7 does answer the question, "How can I have peace in my mind?" Peace in mind comes through the peace of God. Philippians 4:7 says, "And the peace of God, which passeth all understanding, shall keep your hearts and minds through Christ Jesus."

In order to have God's peace, there first needs to be a time in your life when you made peace with God. Romans 5:1 says, "Therefore being justified by faith, we have peace with God through our Lord Jesus Christ." The day you believed in Jesus and received Him as your Lord and Savior marks the day you made peace with God. Oh, happy day!

Have you made peace with God? If so, then you have His peace.

God's Peace versus the Devil's Peace

The Bible calls people who don't believe and trust in Jesus as unbelievers. Unbelievers are not saved, meaning they have never called upon Jesus to save them and be their Savior. They have not made peace with God. I'm sad to say it, but unbelievers aren't part of God's family. Instead, they are part of the devil's family (I John 3:8-10).

The devil does give to his family a generic, imitation type of peace. Jesus said, "Peace I leave with you, my peace I give unto you: *not as the world giveth*, give I unto you. Let not your heart be troubled, neither let it be afraid" (John 14:27) (emphasis mine).

The devil's peace says: "I have no troubles in life. My finances, health, relationships...everything's going great. I'm getting married...having kids...living the dream. I can afford a nice house, car, and travel the world. I can do what I want to do. Ahhhh, life is good and peaceful." Unbelievers believe they have peace when life goes well. Do you see how temporary and generic that kind of peace is?

God's peace says: "Yes, I do have troubles and feel troubled at times, but I'm not anxious because I have God's peace."

Now, I have to admit, I myself have thought: "Nothing major seems to be happening. The bills are paid. The kids are healthy. Yep, everything seems pretty peaceful for us." It's great to have trouble-free times in life, but trouble-free times don't equal God's peace. Despite your circumstances, you can be at peace because you have God's peace!

☑ What does John 14:27 teach about not being troubled or afraid?

GOD HAS GIVEN YOU HIS PEACE SO THERE IS NO NEED TO FEAR.

God's Spirit Produces Peace

Have you ever been through a hard time, but for some amazing reason you felt at peace? Have you ever seen a friend or family member face a trial with deep peace? That's the Holy Spirit's production of it. "To produce" means He's causing it, leading it, and bringing it forward to bear in your life.

Each person of God—the Father, the Son, and the Holy Spirit—demonstrates His connection and character with peace.

☑ God is known as and referred to as the "God of peace" and the "Lord of peace." (Romans 15:33; 2 Thessalonians 3:16)

☑ Jesus is called the "Prince of Peace." (Isaiah 9:6)

☑ The Holy Spirit is the producer of the fruit of peace in your life. (Galatians 5:22)

How come we sometimes don't sense God's peace? How come instead we feel a sinking feeling in the pit of our stomach? How come our mind is full of fears, doubts, worries, and anxieties? How come we don't sense the Holy Spirit?

It's during these times of questions where you can learn a couple things. One, you can't produce your own peace. And two, you are totally reliant upon the Holy Spirit's production of peace in your life. Please understand it's a good thing to be desperate and dependent upon the Holy Spirit's producing of your peace. It's better to leave the producing up to Him than to try to fake it or muster it up on your own.

Did you know that the Holy Spirit can multiply peace? Ooooh, multiplied peace? That's what we all need! Second Peter 1:2 says, "Grace and peace *be multiplied unto you through the knowledge* of God, and of Jesus our Lord" (emphasis mine).

What multiplies your peace? It's the knowledge of God and your Lord Jesus. Wanting peace starts with knowing and learning about Him and His Word. It's a product of your growing relationship with Him. You will know and sense when He's producing peace in your life.

It's an honest struggle for me to explain God's peace because I can't even fully comprehend it myself. Philippians 4:7 says God's peace "passeth all understanding." Have you ever watched a video that claimed to be "Mind Blowing," and it really did blow your mind? In an even greater way, prepare to have your mind blown by God's peace.

What a privilege to have the Spirit produce God's peace in our lives!

☑ How can you start increasing in your knowledge of God?

PRACTACING GRACE AND PEACE THROUGH PRAYER BIBLE READING AND GOING TO CHURCH.

God's Peace Guards

The last part of Philippians 4:7 says God's peace "shall keep your hearts and minds through Christ Jesus." The phrase "shall keep" literally means "to guard." Picture in your mind a war on a battlefield. Guards gather and form on both sides to protect something valuable from the enemy. The guards will do everything it takes to keep their enemies far, far away in order to protect their treasure.

Did you know God's peace patrols as a guard in your mind? Maybe you're thinking, "Wait a minute, Ruth Ann. I thought you're talking about peace. Isn't peace calm, quiet, and relaxing? Why talk about guards, enemies, and war?" Ahhh, herein lies the paradox with peace.

You engage in a mindful battle every day. Knowing God's peace guards your mind helps you understand you have spiritual enemies who want to infiltrate your mind. They can't take away your salvation, but they will do everything they can to rob you of your joy. The devil is a robber who wants to destroy you (John 10:10). When you listen to his lies, you allow them to captivate your thoughts.

The more you understand your mind is a battlefield, the more you will understand your need for God's peace to be your guardian. It's fun to think about guardian angels physically protecting you and your loved ones. It's just as comforting to visualize God's peace guarding and protecting your mind.

Picture a soldier in his barracks and a superior officer walking in the room. Someone yells, "Attention!" The soldier stops everything he's doing, jumps to his feet, clicks his heels, stands tall, puffs out his chest, and gives a salute. He stands at attention!

Here's how God's peace as a guard works:

You allow your mind to go to a place it shouldn't go. A place of fears, doubts, falsehoods, envies, bitterness, anger, immoral thoughts, or anxieties. God's peace enters the room and hollers: "ATTENTION!!!"

What should you choose to do?
☑ Choice #1: Ignore the call to action and keep thinking what you were thinking on.
☑ Choice #2: Listen to the call to action and STOP thinking what you were thinking on. You bring your mind to attention. (Trust me. I know the whole guard-hollering-attention scenario sounds silly, but it really does work!)

It's good to learn and realize what thoughts should not be in your mindful inventory. It's good to also start talking to the Lord. Ask Him for your help, and His forgiveness if need be. You can re-direct your thoughts by prayer, meditation, a favorite song, or verses on a notecard. Find what works best for you.

For me during my swallowing trial, I would look at the Philippians 4:8 refrigerator magnet and verbally quote the verse. I will also admit this battle can be tiresome and time consuming.

Sometimes the enemy gains some ground because you're too tired to deal with it. I speak from experience on this. However, while it seems easier to not bring your mind to "ATTENTION!" it will be harder in the long run; for then you will have more mindful territory to take back and claim.

It is a privilege to have God's Peace support you in your mindful battle.

☑ What are some things you struggle with in your mind?

ANXIETY, DEPRESSION, ANGER

☑ How does God's peace help guard your thinking?

OFFERS COMFORT AND A CALMNESS TO MEDITATE ON.

God's Peace Guides

God's peace does more than guard—it guides. Day in and day out, you need to make decisions, some little and some big. God's peace can guide you to the answers. Colossians 3:15 says, "And let the peace of God rule in your hearts, to the which also ye are called in one body; and be ye thankful."

You are to "let," or allow, God's peace to rule in your heart. The word *rule* means "to govern, preside, to make wise decisions." Like an umpire calls the shots in a ball game, God's peace calls the right shots for your life.

Here are some questions you may have regarding God's will in your life:
- [x] Should I be a member at that church? YES,
- [x] How can I use my talents for the Lord? BEING A HELPER,
- [x] What college should I attend? Or, should I even go to college? DONE,
- [x] Does God want me to take that job? N/A ,
- [x] Should I date/marry him? HMM,
- [x] Should we have another child? NO,
- [x] Is it wise to buy that house? NO,
- [x] Should I quit work? N/A,
- [x] Should I go back to school? MAYBE,
- [x] Should I take or do that treatment? MAYBE.
- [x] Should I retire? NO.
- [x] How can I serve the Lord and others during this season of life? REACH OUT OFF HELP
- [x] Should I paint the bathroom with the leftover yellow color? (*Okay, I know this last one sounds small and silly, but even small questions can drive us crazy!*) NO,

God's peace will guide you. Have you ever prayed and asked God for peace about something, but never sensed peace? I remember praying for peace when I was dating a guy who loved the Lord. Instead, I continued to feel uncomfortable. I later realized God wanted me to feel uneasy; He answered and guided me by *not* giving me peace. Years later, when dating Tim (who's now my husband), I prayed and sensed God's peace. I am forever thankful for the guidance of God's peace.

The last part of Colossians 3:15 says, "...and be ye thankful." You can be thankful to know God's peace guides you in life. It protects you by helping you make life decisions.

☑ Do you have a decision in which you are struggling to make?

WHETHER TO GO BACK TO SCHOOL.

☑ How can God's peace guide and direct you to make decisions?

PRAY TO HIM AND ASK FOR GOD WINKS OR SIGNS I CAN NOTICE.

Here's more good news about God's peace—it patrols on active duty. It's not the retired, ready to relax, time to take a break, and go on a vacation kind. His peace rules as an active, powerful force for you to receive and use. Make sure you thank Him today for His peace in your life!

One last thing. If you know you have not made peace with God but would like to, be sure to read the short chapter at the end of this study called "How to have Peace with God."

Chapter Two

Thinking on Things that are True

*Philippians 4:8: "...whatsoever things are **true**...think on these things."*

Growing up, I loved everything about school. A nerd at heart, I enjoyed learning and studied to ace every class. Whenever I saw a true and false section on a test, I would get excited and play a secret game: *Can Ruth Ann outsmart the test writers?* I felt convinced they stayed up all night, evil laughing "bwahahah," when creating those sneaky questions. Do you know what made the true and false section hard? When the questions or statements contained *both* true and false information.

The day you made peace with God marks the day you received and embarked on a journey for truth. It's no surprise the apostle Paul lists things that are true as the first item on your mindful inventory list. The word *true* comes from a Greek word "alethes" (related to "aletheia") and means "truly, truth, and nothing concealing." God does not hide spiritual truths from you. Actually, He reveals them to you through His Word.

Thinking on spiritual truths helps identify and combat the devil's lies.

In a world bombarded with falsehoods, you can go to Jesus and your Bible as your source of truth. Unfortunately, the devil—the prince of falsehoods, lies, and untruths—shines and excels at taking his lies and mixing them with God's truth.

Truth + Truth = Truth	**False + Truth = False**
Jesus + His Word = Truth	**False + Truth = False**

The mishmash of truth and false produces mixed up minds. I'm not talking about unsaved people; they care less about truth. I'm talking about Christians with the mixed up, confused minds. I know this because I have been there myself, scratching my head and asking, "What's truth?"

Have you ever asked yourself, "What is the truth about _____?" Every time you ask a question, you can find its answer in God's Word. The Holy Spirit will engage; He will help you discover truth. Sometimes He may show you what is false to learn what is true.

Some examples of how biblical truths can overcome the devil's lies:

Ⓧ **Lie from the devil:** *You're not even saved. You don't even remember what you said when you received Jesus as Savior. Maybe you didn't say the right words. You certainly didn't understand everything about Jesus when you trusted in Him.*

☑ **Truth from God's Word:** *I know my heart believed and my mouth confessed. I had childlike faith when I became a child of God. God's Word makes it clear I am saved by grace and through faith.*
~Romans 4:16, 10:9-10; Ephesians 2:1, 8-9; I John 5:13; Mark 10:14-15~

Ⓧ **Lie:** *You have no gifts, no talent. God can't use you.*

☑ **Truth:** *I have the Holy Spirit in my heart and life. I may not know His spiritual gift for me yet, but I do know He has given to me a spiritual gift. I do know God can use me to live and glorify Him.*
~1 Corinthians 12; Ephesians 1:3, 13; Romans 12:3-8; Ephesians 4:7~

Ⓧ **Lie:** *I just can't gain victory over this area in my life. I'm not able to _____. (overcome my fears and anxiety, start a habit of Bible time, quit envying, stop comparing, get over bitterness, quit an addiction, kill a spiritual stronghold in my life...or you fill in the blank.)*

☑ **Truth:** *You are an overcomer through the Lord's victory in your life. His Spirit gives you grace, a supernatural ability, to grow in your walk and relationship with Him.*
~I John 5:4; 1 Corinthians 15:10, 57; I Corinthians 10:13; Colossians 1:10-11~

☑ What are some lies the devil throws at you? What biblical truths do you need to think on to fight and destroy them?

_____

_____

Wearing your Belt of Truth prepares and equips you for battle.

In your spiritual battle, God gives you truth as a weapon. A weapon is "anything used or designed to be used in destroying or annoying an enemy."[2] John 8:32 says, "And ye shall know the truth, and the truth shall make you free." Truth alone doesn't make you free; it's the *knowing of truth* that sets you free.

The apostle Paul mentions truth as the first item in the whole armor of God. "Stand therefore, having your loins girt about with truth..." (Ephesians 6:14). To understand the impact of truth as a weapon, let's look at some of these unfamiliar words along with the biblical culture of the day.

The loins represent the area below your lower ribs to your hip area. The word *girt* means "to gird all around, to tie down, and to fasten on one's belt." You may not be familiar with *girt*, but does the word *girdle* sound familiar? A girdle is an undergarment worn to tuck in and trim the tummy. (I wore one at a wedding to help me fit into a dress. Hopefully that's my last experience with a girdle!)

In Bible times the Jewish people wore girdles, or what you may call a sash. Bible flashcards, movies, or plays display girdles as tied around the waist and hung around one arm and neck. More than an accessory for their robes, the Jewish people wore girdles to hold in their flowing robes and to tie down weapons, money bags, parchments...whatever they needed to carry on their body.

_____

[2] *Noah Webster's 1828 Dictionary.*

Since Paul uses the image of a Roman soldier, the "loins girt about with truth" represents a spiritual weapon—the Belt of Truth. Here's how the Roman soldier's belt equipped him:

☑ *It revealed his preparation and commitment.* The Roman soldier wore a knee-length tunic, a square piece of cloth with holes for the head and arms, with strings that hung off the bottom edges. He wrapped and fastened his belt around the flowy, stringy tunic; he took the tunic strings and tied them down, or girt them, into the belt. Without the belt properly fastened, the tunic and strings would dangle and flap, marking him an easy target for the enemy to pull down. Tightly tucked strings into the belt showed his preparation and commitment. Can you picture him standing tall, wearing his belt, and ready to go to battle?

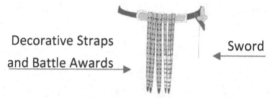

Decorative Straps and Battle Awards ➤   Sword ←

☑ *It kept his sword by his side.* A scabbard, or a sheath, hung off to the side of the belt and held the sword. If a soldier didn't wear his belt, he couldn't have his weapons firmly attached to his body. A soldier without a weapon meant he couldn't properly attack or defend himself. Plus, can you imagine a soldier having to carry his sword during the entire battle? If he did set it down, someone could easily steal it. How cumbersome to carry a sword throughout the entire battle. Battles could last for days, weeks, months, and years.

☑ *It held many decorations and battle awards.* Try to visualize an ornate buckle at the front of the belt with straps dangling down in various shapes of metal and button-doodads. The decorative straps from the belt were designed to say to the enemy, "Look at my accomplishments! Ooooh, you all should be scared of me!"

Here's how the Belt of Truth equips you for today:

☑ *It reveals your preparation and commitment.* By wearing your belt, you are prepared and ready for your mindful battle. With it wrapped and cinched around your waist, your spiritual enemies see you standing and sense your readiness.

☑ *It keeps your Sword by your side.* It is the Belt of Truth that holds your offensive weapon, God's Word, by your side. Do you see how God's truths wrapped and fastened about you keeps your Sword handy? Your spiritual enemies know you will NOT be an open, easy target for them. They know you can both attack and defend.

☑ *It shows your Lord's decorations and battle awards.* Unlike the Roman soldier's belt, yours does not reveal your spiritual accomplishments. It reveals the Lord's accomplishments in your life. It's not, "Oh, look at my belt; look at all I've accomplished. You should all be scared of me." Instead it's, "Oh, look at my belt; look at all the Lord accomplishes in my life. You should all be scared, but not because of me—but because of the Lord and His victory in my life." Your spiritual enemies don't know what you're thinking, but they do know if you are wearing your Belt of Truth!

☑ What does it mean for you to wear the Belt of Truth? How can it help you both defend and attack?

_____

_____

Knowing how to use the Belt of Truth will help you think clearly in your mind.

Did you know the Belt of Truth can help you think clearly? You may experience *brain fog*, a physical condition of confusion, forgetfulness, lack of focus and mental clarity. It can feel frustrating when you don't think clearly. Both brain fog and clear thinking affect you spiritually and physically. I will address the spiritual side of thinking clearly, but I encourage you to also learn the physical side as well.

First Peter 1:13 says, "Wherefore gird up the loins of your mind..." This means you need to tie down and fasten the loose strings, "the loins," of your mind. Where do you gird them? Into your handy dandy Belt of Truth.

Imagine a ball of cooked spaghetti noodles. Each strand represents a thought in your mind, some firm and connected and others soft and loose. Picture the loose strands needing to be cleaned up, tucked in, and tied down. Like a soldier is vulnerable with loose strings hanging from his tunic, you make yourself vulnerable when your mind dangles and tangles into a mess.

What is the key to clearing up loose strings that twist and confuse your thinking? Knowing truth—it gives you the power to think clearly. Here are two loose strings your Belt of Truth can help you think clearly about:

⊗ Sinful Strings

First John 5:17 gives us a biblical definition of sin: "All unrighteousness is sin." Sinful strings can be addictions, strongholds (believing in lies) …basically anything not right in God's eyes. These strings tie around and tie you down. What can help us untangle and clear these out? Knowing and applying Biblical truths. These will help us identify, cut, and confess our sin for a cleansed, clear mind (I John 1:7-8).

⊗ Nagging Strings

These strings contain fear, uncertainty, and indecision. You like to sweep these "under the carpet" because you feel the unknown is better than the known. In the short term, you can get away with shoving the nagging strings aside. For the long term, anxiety and stress will catch up with you. It's time you address and face these nagging strings. In doing so, you may discover dealing with a nagging string to be easier than you thought it would be. It may have taken you more time to keep shoving it away than to actually deal with. Go ahead—locate, identify, snip, and pull those nagging strings away! You will be on your way to thinking with a clearer mind.

☑ How does thinking on lies tangle you up? How can the Belt of Truth set you free?

_____

_____

☑ How does knowing truth help you think with a clear mind?

_____

_____

It's a blessing to know the Belt of Truth helps us fight our mental battles. I hope you see the power of thinking on things that are true. The next time the devil hurls some lies your way, take his lousy true and false test, crumple it up, and throw it back at him. Instead of believing in his lies, allow God's truths to occupy and guard your mind!

Chapter Three
Thinking on Things that are Honest

*Philippians 4:8: "...whatsoever things are **honest**...think on these things."*

When I began to memorize Philippians 4:8, I noticed my Bible's footnote defined the word *honest* as "worthy of respect."[3] Hmmmm...that didn't make much sense to me. That definition sparked something inside me, and I wanted to do more than memorize the verse. I wanted to go deeper in my understanding and study all the "whatsoever things" in the verse.

I'll be honest. This lesson took many different twists and turns. I hope you discover, like I did, how you need honest thinking in your mindful inventory. It affects your relationship with others, how you view yourself, and your relationship with the Lord.

In general, the English word *honest* means "fair or just." In Philippians 4:8, *honest* comes from "middle voice" of a verb in the Greek language. Middle voice means "the subject is both an agent of an action and somehow concerned with the action."[4] Simply put, *honest* in this verse means "honorable and worthy of respect." Honest "points to a Christian decorum...which is quite consistent with true humility, for it is a reverence for the temple of God."[5]

Honest thinking means to think honorable, respectful thoughts about others, you, and the Lord. It's mixed with a blend of humility and a reverence for the temple of God.

---

[3] Charles Ryrie, *Ryrie Study Bible* (Chicago: Moody Publishers, 1994), p. 1800.
[4] https://: Daedalus.umkc.edu Lesson V: Verbs—Introductory, 48. "The Greek verb has three VOICES, the active, middle, and passive."
[5] *Pulpit Commentary*, Philippians 4:8.

You need to think honest thoughts about others.

Have you ever thought something unkind about someone, and you either said it out loud or quietly in your mind? One day I thought about another lady, "She really needs to get it together." Was that an honorable thought? No, it was a dishonest and disrespectful thought. I know; shame on me, right? I never said it out loud, only because I'm careful about things I speak. Maybe you, too, know when to not say dishonest things out loud.

While it can be a good thing to not speak everything on your mind, it's even better to be careful about what you think. You're probably familiar with the saying: "If you can't say something nice, don't say anything at all." I'd like to take that saying a step further: "If you can't think something nice, don't think it at all."

In the sixth grade, I had a friend whose mom called talking bad about others, "trash talk." I remember when she told me and her daughter, "Girls, you need to stop trash talking." I had never heard the phrase *trash talk* before. The more I thought about it, the more I understood the truth in her words. The best way to prevent trash talk is to not have trash thoughts.

Please try to visualize this with me. I have a garbage bag full of yucky trash. Every time I think dishonest and dishonorable things about someone else, the yucky trash bag appears on top of my head. Though I don't see it, you and others do. My trash thoughts make me look (and smell!) bad.

Do you want to be an honest blessing to others? Think honorable thoughts about them. What you think about them inwardly will come out in what you say and how you treat them. People know how you make them feel. No matter how many nice things you may say to someone, you're being insincere and fake when your inner spirit doesn't match your words.

Jesus linked the connection between thoughts and words when He said in Luke 6:45, "A good man out of the good treasure of his heart bringeth forth that which is good; and an evil man out of the evil treasure of his heart bringeth forth that which is evil: *for of the abundance of the heart his mouth speaketh*" (emphasis mine).

To think and speak honest thoughts about others comes when you deposit good things into your heart. Here is why it is best to think honest, respectful thoughts about others—not to prevent you from saying something wrong, but to help you say something right. Your heart and mind influence how you treat other people.

Honest thinking about others shows them a reflection of your spiritual life with the Lord. It reveals a beautiful testimony of a relationship you share with the Lord.

☑ Why is it important to think honest thoughts about others? Why should you remove any dishonest thoughts about others?

_____

_____

You need to think honest thoughts about yourself.

1) Please don't verbally or mentally put yourself down.

Do you constantly put yourself down, either quietly in your mind or out loud? Do you think or say out loud any of these? "I'm ugly. I'm fat. I'm not good enough. I'm old looking. I'm not talented. I'm not like her. I'm not what I used to be like (!). I don't look like how I used to look. I'm not good for anything anymore."

Ladies, it's time you think honest, honorable thoughts about *yourself*! Do you remember, honest thinking is a "reverence for the temple of God"? How you view yourself affects how you view your Creator and temple, the place where the Holy Spirit lives and influences (I Corinthians 3:16).

Obviously, we all have areas in our life in which we can improve. However, I'm talking about when we trash talk and have trash thoughts about ourselves all the time. Remember the yucky garbage bag illustration? Let's look at three things that can consume, fill, and stink up the bag:

⊗ Envy: Proverbs 14:30 calls envy the "rottenness of the bones." Just like we don't want a rotten trash bag staying in our house, we should want to take out of our lives the rottenness of envy.

⊗ Comparing: Second Corinthians 10:12 says we are "not wise" when we compare ourselves to others. On the other hand, wisdom is an "ornament of grace: a crown of glory" (Proverbs 4:9). Hmmm...I know I'd rather wear a crown of wisdom on my head than a trash bag!

⊗ Being unthankful: First Thessalonians 5:18 says it is God's will for us to give thinks "in every thing." A thankful mind and heart is a powerful way to keep trash thoughts and trash talk away.

When you think trash thoughts and speak trash talk about yourself, you plop that bulky bag on your head. Imagine it staying there on you all day while you go throughout your day. While you may not see it, others will. People can know when you're not thinking respectful thoughts about yourself. And even though you can't see the bag, deep down you know it is there.

What should you do when you know the bag is on your head? Remove it! You can start by removing trash thoughts and trash talk out of your mindful inventory. See if there is a pattern to every time you put yourself down; try to prevent yourself from starting up the trash thoughts and trash talk.

This will take intention and time on your part. I can't tell you how many times I have caught myself plopping that bag on my head when getting ready for the day or doing my evening skin care routine.

I searched and searched to find a verse saying we should think less of ourselves. I even speed-read from the beginning of the book of Psalms (since David had his low moments), but I confess to quitting by Psalm 52. I couldn't find even one.

And then it hit me. When we think less of ourselves, when we think ourselves to be of little worth, we think *too much* of ourselves. C.S. Lewis said it best, "Humility is not thinking less of yourself, it's thinking of yourself less."

An honest thinking woman doesn't think too less or too much about herself. Instead, her mind focuses on the Lord and others.

☑ Do you think honest or dishonest thoughts about yourself? How does honest thinking about yourself honor the Lord?

2) Please don't verbally or mentally puff yourself up.

Sometimes you might swing the other way and, instead of putting yourself down, you puff yourself up by thinking you're better than everyone else. You probably know it is easy to come out on top when you compare your strengths to someone else's weaknesses. However, that is not right either; this also includes selfishness, pride, comparing, and boasting.

Honest thinking "points to a Christian decorum...which is quite consistent with true humility." Philippians 2:3-4 says, "Let nothing be done through strife or vainglory; but in lowliness of mind let each esteem other better than themselves. Look not every man on his own things, but every man also on the things of others."

"Lowliness of mind" in the Greek is one big word that means "humbleness of mind." From Philippians 2:3-4, you can ask yourself four questions to see if you have lowliness and humbleness of mind.

☑ Do I have a spirit of strife and contention?

☑ Do I seek personal gain and glory?

☑ Do I respect and honor others?

☑ Do I value and look to the best interest of others?

Colossians 3:12 says, "Put on therefore...humbleness of mind..." The phrase *put on* literally means "to sink into a garment, to invest with clothing, to clothe, to array." How about, instead of putting a yucky trash bag on your head, you put on humbleness of mind? And here's some good news—you get to choose which one you will wear for the day!

You need to think honest thoughts about the Lord.

Did you know your thought life can worship the Lord? The root word for *honest* means "to revere" or "to worship." Honest thoughts about the Lord are "venerable, honorable, and worthy of respect." Honest thinking about the Lord means your thoughts give Him reverence, respect, and worship.

Jesus talked to a Samaritan Woman about worship in John 4:23-24. He said, "But the hour cometh, and now is, when the true worshippers shall worship the Father in spirit and in truth: for the Father seeketh such to worship him. God is a Spirit: and they that worship him must worship him in spirit and in truth."

Jesus desires our *worship,* which means to physically "lay flat, to bow down, to reverence." Many times in the Bible, worship refers to the physical posture. Notice in John 4, Jesus said a true worshipper does *more than* physically bow. A true worshipper bows down before God the Father "in spirit and in truth."

What does that mean? "In spirit" means you connect your spiritual life to the Lord, and "in truth" means the truths you know about God lead you to worship. For example, you will worship Him when you fill your mind with biblical truths about His character, attributes, Word, reputation, testimony, works, majesty, honor…and many others listed from the Bible.

Your mind plays an active role in worship. It discovers, filters, reasons, ponders, discerns, understands, and knows truth. The more truths your mind knows, the more you worship. The more you think honest things about Him, the more you worship both outwardly and inwardly—proving you to be a true worshipper.

When does your thought life not worship the Lord? When you think dishonorable thoughts about others, yourself, and Him. You can't bow before the Lord in worship with a trash bag on your head.

☑ How does honest thinking lead you to true worship?

_____

_____

A lady with honest thinking in her mindful inventory has humbleness of mind. Though she can't see it, she is arrayed, clothed, and wrapped in a beauty that only comes from the Lord. She desires for her mind and life to give honor, respect, and true worship to the Lord.

Chapter Four

Thinking on Things that are Just

*Philippians 4:8: "...whatsoever things are **just**...think on these things."*

I remember an important lesson I learned years ago during Passion Week. At the beginning of the week, I wrote out a list of things to buy: cute dresses for my daughters, find or make matching hair ribbons, search for a new shirt, tie, and vest combo for my son, four pairs of new church shoes, and maybe a necklace for me. I marked my daily calendar with plenty "to do" lists: study and make this lesson for a Facebook live video, find or make a fun object lesson to go with it, practice special music for church, and prepare good food for Good Friday and Easter Sunday. Whew!

It's no wonder by Good Friday I didn't feel too good. Instead, I felt stressed and cranky. I remember scanning an empty section of the little girl tights at Wal-Mart and saying out loud, "This has been a rough week."

In that very moment, the Holy Spirit brought to my mind that my week did not compare to Jesus' suffering during Passion Week. It didn't compare to my friend who found out she had leukemia or the sufferings of other Christians. My "sufferings" came from my over commitments, high expectations, and pride. I quietly asked the Lord to forgive me. I asked Him to help me focus my mind on Him, especially during Passion Week, than on the cares of my little world.

Passion Week is the name for the last week Jesus lived, suffered, and died on earth. Can you imagine the agony He faced that last week of betrayal, rejection, torture, mental anguish, and physical death? We praise Him for His physical resurrection and coming back to life three days later on what we call Easter, or Resurrection Sunday.

Do you know why He died on the cross for you? To justify you, to make you righteous in His eyes, so you can go to heaven. You can't justify yourself; your self-righteousness can't get you into heaven (see Galatians 2:16). The day you believed in Jesus as your Savior marks the day He justified you, and you became just. What an awesome day!

Being justified, He wants you to think on just things. Since we don't use the word *just* and its biblical meaning in our common language, let's learn about it so we can know how to add *just* thinking to our mindful inventory.

A just person can think on just things.

☑ What do the words *just* and *unjust* mean from the Bible?

The dictionary and the biblical definitions for the word *just* contain different meanings. In the dictionary, the word *just* means "to be fair in dealings with people." From Philippians 4:8, the word *just* in the Greek means "righteous." Biblically speaking, just can mean righteous and righteous can mean just. A just person is someone righteous in God's eyes.

An unjust person is someone unrighteous and wicked in God's eyes; someone who has not trusted and received Jesus as their Savior. They don't have to remain in their unrighteousness; they can be justified and made righteous. How? Because Jesus as "the just" died "for the unjust" (I Peter 3:18). By faith they can believe in Jesus and receive His righteousness (Romans 3:22).

☑ What does it mean to be justified?

To be justified means to be made righteous in God's eyes. When you received Jesus, you received His righteousness. Some other names for Jesus include "the Justifier," "the Just One," and "the Just" (Romans 3:26; Acts 7:52; Acts 3:14).

Romans 3:24 and 26 says, "Being justified freely by his grace through the redemption that is in Christ Jesus...To declare, I say, at this time his righteousness: that he (*God*) might be just, and the justifier (*that's Jesus*) of him (*insert your name here!*) which believeth in Jesus."

It's a comfort to know our justification doesn't come by any good thing we do. We don't try to think just thoughts to be justified; we think just thoughts because we are justified.

☑ When did you become justified through Jesus Christ?

WHEN I BELIEVED ON HIM.

☑ How do you add just thoughts in your mind?

To answer this question, let's look from where thoughts come. Webster's 1828 Dictionary says thoughts are "either an act or operation of the mind when thinking on a certain a subject, object, or thing." Your thoughts can be a result from any one of five senses: to see, to feel, to hear, to smell, and to touch.

What you choose, allow, and surround yourself with will influence what you think in your mind. What you choose to *not* allow and surround yourself by will also affect the way you think.

Your experiences (past and present), circumstances, physical health, friends, family, church family, books, social media, videos, music, games, entertainment (this list can go on and on!) all influence and affect your thinking. I find it both a comfort and a challenge to know I can influence my mindful inventory with righteous thoughts.

Here's a list of things to help you think on just things:

☑ Bible reading
☑ friends that sharpen
☑ supportive family members
☑ biblical thoughts
☑ a spiritual journal
☑ meditative verses
☑ a prayer life
☑ books that sharpen
☑ music that uplifts
☑ worship with a church family
☑ supportive social media friends
☑ social media influencers who sharpen you
☑ thought provoking YouTube/online videos

Did you know researchers estimate your mind thinks around 60,000-80,000 thoughts a day? That's an incredible average of 2,500-3,300 thoughts per hour. Other experts estimate a smaller number of 50,000 thoughts per day, which averages to 2,100 thoughts per hour.[6] They believe 80% of your thoughts to be negative while 95-98% of your thoughts are the *same* every day.

Honestly, when I read those statistics I thought, "Oh no! I think around 2,000 thoughts an hour? I'm doomed!" I pictured my mind to be like a bag of microwave popcorn with random kernels of wild, uncontrollable thoughts popping and popping.

I had to stop myself from thinking that, for the truth is we Christians are *not* doomed. We can have victory in our minds to think righteous thoughts. We *do* have the capability, wiring, and spiritual connections to think justly.

☑ What are some things on the list that can help influence you to think on just things?

<u>GO TO CHURCH, READ MY BIBLE, LISTEN TO GODLY MUSIC.</u>

A just person has the mind of Christ.

Before you became justified the Bible says your mind was darkened and ignorant (Ephesians 4:18). Second Corinthians 4:4 says the devil blinds the "minds of them which believe not."

---

[6] www.successconsciousness.com, Remez Sasson, "How Many Thoughts Does Your Mind Think in One Hour?"

Have you ever wondered: "How come some people don't understand about_____ (abortion, church fellowship, purity, serving, giving, Bible time, etc.)?" It's because unbelievers can't understand righteous things. First Corinthians 2:14 says they can't receive "the things of the Spirit of God: for they are foolishness unto him: neither can he know them, because they are spiritually discerned."

I have read through my Bible and the book of First Corinthians many times. When I began this study, I came across a verse I felt like I had never read before. First Corinthians 2:16 says, "For who hath known the mind of the Lord, that he may instruct him? But we have the mind of Christ."

Wait, what? The mind of Christ? I, we, have His mind? The mind which helped Him fulfill the Father's will? Yes, to each of these! If you're justified, He has given to you His mind as well. You have the mind of Christ.

Have you ever wondered, "How could Jesus endure and go through all that He did?" I believe one answer comes from Philippians 2:5. It says, "Let this mind be in you, which was also in Christ Jesus." His mind influenced Him to live a sacrificial life, "even to the death of the cross" (Philippians 2:8). His mind gave Him victory in His life, and His mind gives you victory in yours.

Has someone ever given you a gift, but you didn't know how to use it? Or, maybe you didn't want to use it in order to keep it preserved? When Jesus left the earth, He left behind a gift, a legacy, for all who believe in Him—His mind. It isn't a gift for you to stuff in the darkest part of your closet nor to display on a prominent shelf. It's a gift He gives you to use.

Knowing you have the mind of Christ will help you know you *can* think on just things. You will discover you *can* have victory in your mind and in your life. You will also feel motivated to use this amazing God-given gift to think on just things.

Jesus wants you to use His mind to full capacity. Here's two things His mind gives you: spiritual understanding and spiritual perception.

☑ Spiritual understanding

Spiritual understanding isn't something magical. It simply means you understand spiritual things about the Lord and His Word. The more you read His Word, the more His mind activates your understanding. Luke 24:45 says, "Then opened he their understanding, that they might understand the scriptures." Jesus knew His disciples needed understanding in order to preach the gospel. He knows you, too, need understanding today as well.

☑ Spiritual perception

Not to brag or anything, but I have a gift of perception—with ice cream! I can look at different kinds and tell you which one will taste the best according to its smoothness, color, and texture! Okay, I know that sounds silly, but it helps illustrate perception.

Spiritual perception is seeing, knowing, and sensing the Holy Spirit's guidance. Jesus perceived (Matthew 16:8; Mark 2:8; Luke 5:22; John 6:15), and you can have spiritual perception as well. You can spiritually perceive: people's needs, sin and its dangers, your spiritual enemies, your gifts, others gifts, how to use them, and the love of God (I John 3:16).

It's a blessing to know you have the mind of Christ. Knowing you have His mind will give you strength in your mind. When Jesus lived here on earth, you were on His mind. May you use His mind while you live here on earth!

☑ How does knowing you have the mind of Christ give you strength in your mind?

IT TEACHES ME TO ENDURE EVEN WHEN I AM SUFFERING

It is good to not think about things you shouldn't, but it is better to think on things you should. Just things, along with all the other items on the inventory list from Philippians 4:8, won't naturally pop into your mind throughout the day—they need to be intentional.

42

A just thinking woman finds her confidence in Christ. She knows she is justified, and she uses the mind of Christ to think on just things.

Don't you feel so blessed to know you're justified, made righteous, in God's eyes? It is a privilege and a comfort to know the Lord gives us many resources—His Word, His Spirit, His peace guardian, and His Mind—to help us think on just things.

Chapter Five

Thinking on Things that are Pure

*Philippians 4:8: "...whatsoever things are **pure**...think on these things."*

Imagine I invite you to my house for coffee or tea. You pick from my cupboard the cup you like best. I take the mug and make a dramatic display of shining the outside. We chuckle as I hand you the sparkly mug. To your horror, the inside is full of mold and muck! Would you want me to pour your drink into it? I don't think so. No matter how sparkly or clean the outside is, you would want the inside to be clean.

Jesus had a dining experience with a Pharisee, a religious man who sought to look good on the outside. Luke 11:37-38 says, "And as he spake, a certain Pharisee besought him to dine with him: and he went in, and sat down to meat. And when the Pharisee saw it, he marvelled that he had not first washed before dinner."

Jesus wasn't against washing hands. He was against the ceremonial pomp and display the Pharisees did when they washed their hands. Jesus said, "Now do ye Pharisees make clean the outside of the cup and the platter; but *your inward part is full* of ravening and wickedness" (Luke 11:39) (emphasis mine).

What a great illustration to show the hypocrisy of looking good on the outside while the inside is full of filthiness. Looking good on the outside while neglecting the inside only produces a life for display. A life full of purpose and productivity for the Lord and others works on its inner condition.

Philippians 4:8 tells us to think on pure things. The word *pure* means to be clean, to be unmixed with something else that would taint it. When adding together something pure to impure, or vice versa, it becomes tainted and impure.

Do you want a pure mind? You need to take ownership of its care and maintenance. You may wish your mind came with a self-cleaning button like a new oven, but it has something even better—the cleansing power of the Lord. Rest assured, He will help you through the process of thinking on and keeping a pure mind.

What impure thoughts are filling up your mind?

⊗ Dirty thoughts

These are immoral, inappropriate thoughts, like secret fantasies and imaginations. I believe you know what I'm talking about.

Sometimes you may deceive yourself into thinking it is harmless for your mind to go to a dirty place. Have you ever thought the following? *No one else can know what I'm thinking, so it's no big deal. I can think whatever I want. My personal life is just that—personal. It only concerns me and no one else; it won't harm anyone else. After all, it's all in my mind and just stays in my mind. Nothing more.*

The Bible has a verse for this kind of thinking. Proverbs 23:7 says, "For as he thinketh in his heart, so is he." You become what you think. A dirty mind produces dirty actions. The good news is Proverbs 23:7 can go another way. A pure mind produces pure actions. Your mind can be a public testimony to others about the Lord and His Word's cleansing power in your life.

☑ How can dirty thoughts affect others around you?

_____

_____

⊗ Doubtful thoughts

Doubtful thoughts can nag, consume, haunt, and bog us down. You can shove them to the back of your mind and hope they will magically disappear. However, when left undealt with, they will creep their way back to their haunting place in the front of the mind.

Remember the story of Peter walking on the water to Jesus? Once Peter took his eyes off Jesus and saw the "wind boisterous," Peter began

46

to sink; He cried, "Lord, save me." Jesus replied, "O thou of little faith, wherefore didst thou doubt?" (Matthew 14:30-31). This shows that you can believe in Jesus, indeed be a close follower of His, and still doubt Him.

Years ago, I had serious doubts and questions about a major biblical event. I made a poster board, sticky notes, family tree, and a timeline. I scoured books and emailed questions to pastors and Bible scholars. God used that time of doubt to help me learn and grow in my faith. I gained a whole new respect for the Bible and how history proves its accuracy. Doubts, when properly dealt with, can help you grow in your faith.

However, when left undealt, doubts will cause anxiety, worry, and stress. The more they stew and rot in your mindful inventory, the more your mind becomes clouded and tainted.

What should you do when you have doubts?

- ☑ Stop and address any that come to mind.
- ☑ Write them down. I highly recommend keeping a notebook throughout this process.
- ☑ Pray and talk to the Lord about your doubts. Ask Him to guide you and to bring truth to light.
- ☑ Turn to your Bible, spiritual leaders, respected Bible teachers, wise family and friends to help you.
- ☑ Write down evidences and biblical truths as you connect the puzzle pieces along the way.
- ☑ Pray again. Keep the lines of communication open with the Lord.

With the Lord's help, you can transform your doubts from a panic, to a process, to a confidence.

- ☑ What are some doubtful thoughts you struggle with, and what steps can help you deal with them?

_____

_____

Ⓧ Destructive thoughts

Destructive thoughts destroy us spiritually, mentally, and physically. They build, consume, entangle, burn, and bring harm to you and others around you. Here are some types: bitterness, envy, anger, comparing, discontentment, unforgiveness, and pride.

I remember a time when I didn't know I had destructive thoughts. I attended a teacher's conference, of all things, when I heard a message from the life of Joseph. The Holy Spirit used that sermon to show me I had allowed bitterness to fill up, entangle, and burn me up. Later that night I shared my new discovery with my closest friend. I'll never forget her reaction. She said, "I know." Wait…how could she know what I myself had learned hours earlier?

Destructive thoughts need to be dealt with; they need to be destroyed. Second Corinthians 10:5 gives us some insight. It says, "Casting down imaginations…and bringing into captivity every thought to the obedience of Christ."

The phrase "casting down" means "to kill first, then lower and demolish." (An example would be from Acts 13:29 when the Jews lowered Jesus' dead body from the cross to the grave.) "Bringing into captivity" literally means "to take every thought captive with a spear." You then take these dead thoughts and, in obedience, present them to your Commander.

This process sounds gruesome and tiresome, and it is. Your whole battle in your mind will take intention, attention, time, energy, and God's grace. In your real spiritual battle with the devil and his spiritual forces, you don't want your enemy to destroy you. Why would you allow your own thoughts to destroy you?

☑ How does Second Corinthians 10:4-5 give us weapons to help us destroy any destructive thoughts?

_____

_____

How can you cleanse and purify your mind?

Please understand you *can* clean up your impure mind. Let's continue the conversation Jesus had with the Pharisee in Matthew 23:26. He said, "Thou blind Pharisee, *cleanse first that which is within* the cup and platter, that the outside of them may be clean also" (emphasis mine).

As a Christian, you are ultimately cleansed from your sin and should desire to keep yourself clean and pure. "Having therefore these promises, dearly beloved, *let us cleanse ourselves from all filthiness of the flesh and spirit,* perfecting holiness in the fear of God" (2 Corinthians 7:1) (emphasis mine).

Remember the mucky mug illustration? Let's say I take your dirty cup and pour a few splashes of purified water into it. Purified water should do the trick, right? Except now the small splashes make it muddier. Adding a few pure thoughts to your mind doesn't instantly mean "presto!"—your mind is pure.

Cleansing comes from a heartfelt conversation with God. Look what David asked the Lord in Psalm 51:2. "Wash me throughly from mine iniquity, and cleanse me from my sin." Do you see David asked the Lord to both "wash" and "cleanse" him? The word *wash* means "to trample…by stamping with the feet" and *cleanse* means "to be pure."

Please don't panic at how complicated and messy this sounds. It's not easy, but it is simple. When you give the Lord your impure mind, it's like you're handing Him a dirty mug. He is the One who does the washing and cleansing.

What happens if I submerge the dirty mug into a deep basin full of several gallons of water?

Plunge into the water: "Lord, here's my mind."

Splash! "It's time I talk to You about_____."

Swirl: "Please forgive me for _____."

Swoosh: "I need Your grace, Your cleansing in my life."

Hey, it's starting to get clean! Ahhhh, don't you feel better with a cleaner mind? It still may contain tainted spots; but thanks to the Lord's cleansing process, your mind is purer and cleaner.

☑ Write down a personal prayer asking the Lord for a pure mind, trusting His grace to help you with the process.

_____

_____

What are pure things I am to think on?

At first glance this question sounds easy to answer. However, I have found it to be most thought provoking. I easily found Bible verses that talk about impure things, but nothing quite so clear that reference pure things— except about the Lord Himself and His Word. This led me to wonder: *Are pure things only about the Lord and His Word or can thinking on pure things be about other things?*

I went back to the meaning of pure to give me a clean start (pun intended!). The Greek word for *pure* is "hagios," and it means "pure from defilement, not contaminated, innocent, chaste, modest, and clean." From there, I followed and connected the dots to the Holy ("hagios") Spirit (or Ghost).

This became my "Aha!" moment. Pure thoughts come from a pure source!

☑ Knowing pure things come when we know our Lord.
☑ Knowing pure things come when we know His Word.

To add pure things doesn't mean you have to binge read or memorize your Bible all day long. It means the source of your thoughts comes from pureness. For example, it's a pure thing to think, "I love my family." The Bible doesn't literally say to "love your family," but the principles on loving your family come from the life of Jesus and fellow believers throughout the Bible. Loving your family comes from loving the Lord— and that's pure.

To help you better understand pure things, here are three questions you can ask:

☑ *Is this an impure thought?* Sometimes identifying impure things can help us identify pure things.

☑ *Would Jesus think this?* He is a holy God.

☑ *What's a biblical principle or source to help me better identify this thought?*

☑ Write down any additional questions you think can help you understand pure things.

_____

_____

I'm sure you see the time, energy, and maintenance that goes into a clean mind. I hope you also see its benefits and blessings. A pure mind enjoys its communion and connection with the presence of the Holy Spirit.

A godly Christian lady desires purity in her mind. She gladly embraces and commits to the cleansing process that will take her an entire lifetime!

Chapter Six

Thinking on Things that are Lovely

*Philippians 4:8: "...whatsoever things are **lovely**... think on these things."*

Have you ever gone through a time where it felt you had a black cloud hover over you? Whether a spiritual shadow, gloom, fog, haze, or even a storm—it seemed to weigh and press you down. I remember the time a black cloud hovered over me. It covered me with thoughts of doom and gloom, blocking any rays of light. I wanted it to go away, but I didn't know how to shake it off.

Do you know what helps get rid of those spiritual dark clouds? Thinking on lovely things. Do you know what causes those dark clouds to gather, form, spread, and hover? Thinking on unlovely things. Both lovely and unlovely thoughts are powerful; they affect how you view the Lord and how you live your life.

The word *lovely* from Philippians 4:8 appears only once in the New Testament. It comes from the Greek word "prosphiles" which means "friendly towards, acceptable, and pleasing." Though these meanings sound sweet and simple, make no mistake about the power with lovely thinking.

What are lovely thoughts? Thoughts that are friendly. They give security, confidence, support, strength, growth, health, and help you thrive. They take you to a place of hope, comfort, relief, peace, renewal, healing, and strength.

What are unlovely thoughts? Thoughts that are unfriendly. They give you no support and no strength. These thoughts weaken and discourage you. They will weigh you down and zap you mentally, spiritually, and physically.

Do you want a lovely mind? Are you ready to learn the power with lovely thinking? Here are three things you can do:

☑ Identify and remove any unlovely things that form and darken your mind.

☑ Replace with lovely things to give you a breakthrough and hope.

☑ Know and think on lovely biblical truths and verses to give you a lovely mind. You may find some of your favorite Bible verses are lovely; for they give you strength, comfort, healing, and hope.

Here are some examples of lovely Bible verses ~Isaiah 40:31; Psalm 23; Joshua 1:8-9; Psalm 46:1,10; Matthew 6:25-34; 2 Timothy 1:7~

☑ What lovely verses give you strength, comfort, healing, and hope?

_____

_____

Let's look at two examples of unlovely and lovely thinking, along with some lovely Bible verses.

☑ Unlovely thoughts: *I feel guilt and condemnation, and sometimes I don't even know why. Everything seems to be doom and gloom in my mind.*

☑ Lovely thoughts: *I am neither guilty nor condemned in God's eyes. When I do something wrong, His Spirit convicts me to make things right again. His conviction helps me to think clearly and have a lovely mind.*

Romans 8:1-2 says: "There is therefore now no condemnation to them which are in Christ Jesus, who walk not after the flesh, but after the Spirit. For the law of the Spirit of life in Christ Jesus hath made me free from the law of sin and death."

Have you ever felt guilty about something, but couldn't pinpoint why? Maybe you have thought: "I'm a lousy friend. I'm not a good wife. I'm a bad mom. I don't deserve to have my wonderful family. I'm not worthy to have this job. My life doesn't matter anymore. I should just give up. I can't do anything right. I'm not good enough. I feel like God doesn't care. God won't forgive me. God won't ever use me again."

Do you know what happens when you think these unlovely things? You condemn yourself by pronouncing yourself guilty. Your condemnation starts the formation of little black clouds.

Not only do you condemn yourself, but your enemy Satan also tries to condemn you. Notice I said *tries*, for he has no power to declare any Christian guilty. Romans 8:1 declares anyone "in" Christ Jesus has *no* condemnation. Having *no* condemnation, you should not live or think in condemnation.

There will be times when you know you said, thought, or did something wrong and need to make things right with the Lord. That's called conviction. Though the word *conviction* is not in the KJV, there are 17 references in the New Testament that come from the Greek word "elegcho," which means "to convict, convince, reprove, tell a fault." We use the word *conviction* to specify when the Lord speaks, reproves, and reminds us of a fault (see John 16:7-8).

Conviction from the Holy Spirit is lovely thinking. Conviction is specific, while condemnation is general. Here's a comparison:

- ☑ Conviction—a specific thought: "It was wrong of me to lose my temper and scream at my kids. I need to ask them to forgive me."
- ⊗ Condemnation—a general thought: "I'm a bad mom."

I hope you see the difference between conviction and condemnation. It's a lovely thing to make things right with the Lord when He specifically convicts us. A lovely mind doesn't allow guilt to form black clouds. It loves to clear the air!

- ☑ Can you think of a re-occurring condemning thought you struggle with? Is there something the Holy Spirit is convicting you about to make right with Him?

_____

_____

⊗ Unlovely thoughts: *I feel so depressed and discouraged. I have no strength. Things feel so hopeless.*

☑ Lovely thoughts: *I will remember the goodness of God and my hope in Him. His mercy and compassion never fail, for they are new every morning. Great is His faithfulness!*

Let's look at how Jeremiah, a prophet in the Old Testament, dealt with feelings of no strength, no hope, and depression. It is reassuring to know, someone who heard directly from God felt depressed.

God spoke messages to Jeremiah, who in turn delivered them to his fellow Israelites. The Israelites did not listen to nor heed his messages. Instead, they turned their backs on God and toward idol worship. God allowed the mighty King Nebuchadnezzar and his Babylonian army to besiege Jerusalem for a year, causing the Jewish people to starve. Nebuchadnezzar tore down the city walls, stole from the temple, burned the city, and deported prisoners to Babylon.

During this time, Jeremiah felt "pressed to the point of despair."[7] After witnessing his beloved country's fall, Jeremiah mourned and wrote down his sorrows.

"And I said, My strength and my hope is perished from the LORD: Remembering mine affliction and my misery, the wormwood and the gall. My soul hath them still in remembrance, and is humbled in me" (Lamentations 3:18-20).

Did you know the word *affliction* here means depression? *Misery* has the idea of being an outcast; *wormwood* and *gall* were poisonous plants known to be odious, bitter, and harmful. Then, somewhere at the end of verse 20, Jeremiah began to remember his Lord. He felt humbled, which means he literally sank and bowed before the Lord. While on his knees in worship, he brought to his mind lovely thoughts.

---

[7] Charles Ryrie, *Ryrie Study Bible* (Chicago: Moody Publishers, 1994), p.1178.

"This I recall to my mind, therefore have I hope. It is of the LORD'S mercies that we are not consumed, because his compassions fail not. They are new every morning: great is thy faithfulness" (Lamentations 3:21-23). What helped Jeremiah? Thinking about the Lord, His testimony, mercies, compassions, renewal, and faithfulness.

Wow, such a beautiful example of the power of lovely thinking!

☑ Do you or someone you know struggle with depression? How can thinking lovely things give you hope and healing in your mind?

_____

_____

Let's talk about Depression. It's derived from a Latin verb that literally means "to press down." The word *depression* may mean something different to you than someone else.

⊗ It may mean a week or month full of challenges.

⊗ It may represent a tough time you went through for a short season.

⊗ It may represent several seasons or years.

⊗ It may seem to never have an end.

Whatever your level or definition of depression is, I think we can agree it's an unlovely thing to go through. Please don't misunderstand me. I'm not saying we should never feel down or discouraged. Feelings of depression, discouragement, weakness, and hopelessness can come and go. However, I'm talking about the times when you feel pressed down to the point of despair. Your black cloud seems to never let up.

When I went through my swallowing trial, Tim and I called it a nervous breakdown. I had anxiety and panic attacks. Physically I felt weak, due to lack of proper nutrition. I didn't want to go out or be around people; I just wanted to stay in my room. I didn't realize until later, I went through a time of depression.

Depression is real and not something we can just "get over" and "snap out of." Depression means the mind is broken and needs to heal.[8] In my

_____

[8] John Morrow, an independent Baptist pastor, from a sermon called "Ways to Help Someone Get through Depression" (at New Testament Baptist Church, Feb. 21. 2021).

case, a traumatic physical experience brought it on. High levels of stress can bring on high levels of anxiety, which can bring on depression.

How did I get out of my depression? First, my husband Tim supported me throughout my healing. After I could swallow, he told me to take every afternoon off to relax. He did everything that I normally did for the kids and with the house. Second, I would go to my happy place—sitting on our back deck in the Arizona sunshine—with my Bible, notebook, pen, paper, lemon tea in a mason jar, and, most of the time, nachos. It felt wonderful to chew and swallow again!

What happened almost every afternoon? I would study Philippians 4:8 and then end with a nap. I know the nap sounds unspiritual, but those peaceful afternoons helped me to heal. The more I learned from Philippians 4:8 and rested, the more my mind seemed to come back to life. It took me a few months for my panic attacks to go away. My depression, my black cloud, seemed to lift higher and scatter with each day. Thank You, Lord!

I say this to encourage you if you struggle with anxiety, depression, panic attacks, and/or just feeling pressed down. You can experience mental healing. Your mind can heal. Don't accept depression as a part of your new normal. Instead, make it a top priority to find and attain healing in your mind, both spiritually and physically.

Am I saying lovely thoughts and verses will cure you of depression? No, but they are a powerful place to start. When you feel your black cloud press you down, ask yourself: "What am I thinking on?" Then ask yourself, "What do I *need* to be thinking on?"

☑ Have you ever sensed a black cloud hover over you from time to time? If so, what are some things you can do to chase it away?

_____

_____

As ladies, we love lovely things like decorations, clothes, accessories, food, drinks, vacations, and scenery. May we also desire to have a lovely mind!

Chapter Seven

Thinking on Things of a Good Report

*Philippians 4:8: "...whatsoever things are of a **good report**... think on these things."*

Has someone ever told you something that either made your day or hurt you deeply? Last summer my family and I volunteered to help out at our favorite Christian camp. The camp cook and I met up in the kitchen, and she shared with me something my son Hardy told her four years earlier. He had said, "You cook as good as you look, and you look pretty good." She told me his words touched her so much she wrote them down in a journal. I said, "Words are powerful," and she nodded her head in agreement.

This lesson will show how your mind influences your words, which reveal your thoughts and beliefs. Your words can inspire and give courage, or discourage and stir up fear. Good report thinking affects you and your testimony, others and their testimonies, and the Lord and His testimony. It will give Him glory!

The phrase *good report* means: "well spoken of, reputable, of a good reputation." It's a "tendency to maintain a good name... that which may be for the honour of Christ, and the reputation of the gospel..."[9]

Good report thinking means you think good things in your mind about the Lord, His name, His honor, and His reputation. To help you understand good report thinking, I would first like you to see the other side of the coin, the opposite—evil report thinking.

---

[9] *Matthew Poole's Commentary on the Holy Bible*, Philippians 4:8.

Evil Report Thinking

Unfortunately, we don't always think good reports about our Lord. An evil report is "slander, a false report, and a total loss of reputation." This thinking may sound extreme to you and something a mature Christian wouldn't do. However, you may discover, like I did about myself, there have been times you either knowingly or unknowingly did not think a good report about the Lord.

Evil report thinking can simply mean the Lord has lost His reputation in your eyes. Instead of feeling amazed by His amazingness, you feel distrust towards Him.

You can learn about evil report thinking from the Israelite people in Numbers 13. God told Moses to send 12 men, one from each tribe, to search the Promised Land. Moses sent them to spy on the land and the people to see "whether they be strong or weak, few or many" (Numbers 13:18).

Moses also wanted a full report of the land and cities, the comforts and the perks. He requested they bring back fruit samples of the land—yes, please! Forty days later the spies returned with a huge cluster of grapes that hung between two staffs, along with pomegranates and figs. However, along with the mixed fruit they brought mixed reviews.

Standing before Moses and all the congregation of the children of Israel, the ten spies began their report. In the first opening sentence, they acknowledged the land's fruitfulness (Numbers 13:27). From their second sentence to beyond, they labeled the people as giants, the cities walled, and the land surrounded by enemies.

Two good spies named Joshua and Caleb saw the people's horror. Caleb tried to calm them down. He said, "Let us go up at once, and possess it; for we are well able to overcome it" (Numbers 13: 30).

The 10 spies quickly disagreed. "We be not able to go up against the people; for they are stronger than we. *And they brought up an evil report*" (emphasis mine) (Numbers 13:31-32). Oh, how sad these ten spies, who had personally witnessed God's glory in Egypt and the wilderness (Numbers 14:22), brought up an evil report.

Why? It's because they didn't have good report thinking in their minds. They had forgotten their Lord, His name, His honor, and His reputation.

Here are some examples of evil report thinking about the Lord:

⊗ *I know He was with me in the past, but I don't know if He is with me now.*

⊗ *I know God wants me to claim victory in this battle, but I don't know if He will help me do it.*

⊗ *I know the Lord has given to me the Promised Land of heaven. I don't know if I can fully trust Him to help me overcome my giants while I live here on earth.*

Whoa, do you see the distrust for God even though you did trust Him at one time? Evil report thinking leads you to thinking false things about the Lord.

☑ What has the Lord done for you in your life? How can remembering Him and His reputation keep you from thinking an evil report about Him?

_____

_____

Evil Report Speaking

Can you picture all the drama that followed with millions of Israelites speaking, murmuring, crying, and conspiring? As they started to make death threats, "the glory of the LORD appeared in the tabernacle of the congregation before all the children of Israel" (Numbers 14:10).

After a lengthy conversation with Moses, God told Moses "...all the earth shall be filled with the glory of the LORD. Because all those men which have seen my glory, and my miracles...Surely they shall not see the land..." (Numbers 14:21-23).

How sad these people who had seen God's glory in the past—the ten plagues, the miracles, the parting of the Red Sea, God's deliverance, His provision in the wilderness—couldn't see how God could do it for them again. What happened? They didn't remember God's powerful reputation.

Evil report thinking takes place in your mind. It happens when you—
- ⊗ Forget the Lord's name, reputation, and miracles in your life—instead of remembering and reminding yourself about Him.
- ⊗ Focus on your weaknesses—instead of trusting the Lord to give you strength during weakness.
- ⊗ Obsess about your enemies' strengths—forgetting God's plan and promises in your life.

☑ How does evil report thinking affect you and your testimony along with others and their testimonies?

_____

_____

Do you see the good news? You get to choose what you think. You can choose to *not* think evil reports. You *can* think on things of a good report.

Good Report Thinking

We all love to hear things of a good report spoken from a doctor, teacher, pastor, friend, or family member. Proverbs 15:30 says, "The light of the eyes rejoiceth the heart: and a good report maketh the bones fat." Hearing good tidings can sink all the way deep down in our bones.

When you think good reports about the Lord, it means you think well of Him. The more you think well of Him, the more you will personally know Him. The more you personally know Him, the more you will think well of Him. They circle back and around to each other!

Here's three attributes about God to remind you of His amazingness. Knowing and believing these things about Him will help you think well of Him:

1) He's omniscient. Omniscience means the Lord knows all things. Omni means "all," and science means "knowledge." He knows where you are, where you are headed, and where you need to be. You can trust Him because He knows everything!

~Psalm 139:1-5: "Thou knowest my downsitting and mine uprising, thou understandest my thought afar off. Thou compassest my path and my lying down, and art acquainted with all my ways. For there is not a word in my tongue, but, lo, O LORD, thou knowest it altogether." ~

2) He's omnipresent. Omnipresence means the Lord's presence is everywhere in your life. He goes before you, behind you, and beside you. Also, remember the Holy Spirit lives inside you. Wherever you go, and whatever you go through, God goes with you.

~Psalm 139:7-8: "Whither shall I go from thy spirit? or whither shall I flee from thy presence? If I ascend up into heaven, thou art there: if I make my bed in hell, behold, thou art there." ~

3) He's omnipotent. Omnipotence means the Lord's all powerful. He has unlimited power, and His love for you is all powerful and unlimited as well. He gave you life, and the Holy Spirit gives you power in your life.

~Psalm 139:13-14, 17: "For thou hast possessed my reins: thou hast covered me in my mother's womb. I will praise thee; for I am fearfully and wonderfully made: marvellous are thy works; and that my soul knoweth right well...How precious also are thy thoughts unto me, O God! how great is the sum of them!" ~

☑ Which attribute about Him encourages you to think good reports about Him?

_____

_____

Good Report Speaking

Do you ever talk to yourself? I do. I especially used to talk to myself when I was single. One time, when Tim and I were dating long distance and talking on the phone, he told me, "I don't mind you talking to yourself. But when we talk on the phone, can you try to only talk to me?" I laughed and assured him I would work on that.

I know this may sound silly, but try talking to yourself *out loud* good words about the Lord. These don't need to be shouted, since you are the speaker and listener. You may find yourself preferring to whisper them, like whispering a prayer.

I love what Shelly Hamilton wrote on Facebook. She said, "Speak truth to yourself. As my son-in-law Ben tells me, 'Don't listen to yourself, talk to yourself.'"[10]

Aren't you glad it's okay to talk to yourself? I am!

Here are some sample whisperings:

✓ Lord, I know You are mine, and I am Yours.

✓ You are my Savior for eternal life, and I can trust You with my earthly life.

✓ You created time, and I trust Your timing to be best in my life.

✓ Your Spirit lives in me, and I can trust Your presence to comfort and strengthen me."

✓ You and Your name need to be honored and glorified. I want my life to give You honor and glory.

✓ What good report do you need to talk or whisper *out loud* to yourself about the Lord today?

_____

_____

---

[10] Shelly Hamilton, author and musician from Majesty Music, January 36, 2021: "Defeating the 'Fake Voices' (cont. from post, 01/25)".

Good Report Thinking and Speaking
Gives Glory to God

The apostles Peter and John healed a lame man and boldly spoke good reports about "Jesus Christ of Nazareth" (Acts 3:6). This angered some religious leaders, who commanded Peter and John to not speak about Jesus. They replied, "For we cannot but speak the things which we have seen and heard" (Acts 4:20). They said they couldn't help but speak a good report.

The religious leaders issued a stern warning, but released Peter and John "because of the people: for all men glorified God for that which was done" (Acts 4:21). Yes, the miracle no doubt amazed them; but so did the testimony of God's power in Peter and John's lives. They gave God all the glory!

Do you ever make spiritual goals? Years ago, I wrote down a spiritual goal: *for my life to glorify God.* While studying this lesson, I added on to it: *and for my mind and mouth to glorify God.* Romans 15:6 says, "That ye may with one mind and one mouth glorify God."

To give God glory means to give His name honor and reputation. This results in people seeing Him in all His glory. Hmmm…giving God glory sound similar to good report thinking!

☑ How can you use your mind and mouth to glorify the Lord?

_____

_____

It's apparent we can't separate our minds from our mouths. They both connect and work together to be a part of glorifying God. As we think on things of a good report, may we glorify Him!

Chapter Eight
Thinking on Things of Virtue

*Philippians 4:8: "...if there be any **virtue**...*
think on these things."

Do you remember all the confusion and challenges we experienced in the year of 2020? From Covid, toilet paper shortages, school cancellations, quarantine, food shortages, masks, hand sanitizer by the gallon, deaths of loved ones, conflicting information, a dramatic election...what a strange time! We certainly saw the crazy people come out of the woodwork.

Do you know what else I saw? I saw the crazy come out in me! My mind felt confused, weak, and tired. I knew I needed strength in my mind. I kept thinking, "I want a strong mind. How can I have strength of mind?"

How can we have a strong mind? By thinking on things that strengthen our minds—things of virtue.

In Philippians 4:8, I love how the word *virtue* comes from the Greek word *arête* (pronounced "air-uh-tay"). The ancient Greeks used arête to describe things in different ways. For example, to call a knife arête meant it cut strong, sharp, and excellent. To call someone arête meant they lived a life of virtue with strength, bravery, courage, manliness, valor, moral goodness, knowledge, a life to be praised, and a life of excellence.

From these many definitions for virtue, three caught my eye: strength, courage, and excellence. A virtuous mind thinks with strength and courage to live a life of excellence.

1) You need Christian virtue to strengthen your mind.

You may wonder if you can think virtuous thoughts. I'm here to say as a Christian you can, for even unbelievers can. Many claim their strength comes from within themselves, worldly philosophies, good morals, positive thinking, inspirational quotes, physical fitness, support systems, etc. While these virtues do produce temporary strength in life, they're not sustainable. They will come and go.

A Christian woman desires more than to excel, to be good, to do good to others, to have a good quality life, and to live by an ethical/moral code. She desires a healthy, strong mind to live a virtuous life for the Lord.

Have you heard the phrase *mental health*? It seems to be everywhere on Facebook, YouTube, magazine covers at the checkout stands, and even pop-up ads on Google. It's now the month of May, and a few weeks ago I heard May is "Mental Health Awareness Month."

I'm all for mental health. But as Christians, let us go a step farther and talk about mental strength. It may sound the same as mental health, but it's not. A healthy mind enjoys being sound and content, while a strong mind produces energy and force. For example, a healthy mind does not give in to fears while a strong mind conquers its fears. Do you see the difference?

Though we still may need to work on our mental health (I know I do!), let's not stop there. Let's pursue having mental strength. Mental strength is a process, a journey—not a destination. A virtuous mind desires to be healthy and strong!

Here are some ABC's of virtuous thinking to help strengthen your mind:

a) Ask the Lord to give you mental strength. I know this sounds basic, but I believe it's the first step to both mental health and mental strength. Share your heart with the Lord by asking Him to heal and strengthen your mind. David said in Psalm 138:3, "In the day when I cried thou answeredst me, and strengthenedst me with strength in my soul."

b) Believe your mind can be strong—no matter your past mental history, physical health issues, and personal limitations. Last year I thought, *I wish my mind could go back to normal; the way it was before my health trial.* Maybe you, too, wish you could go back to a "normal" time in your life. Remember, you have the mind of Christ, which means you have the wiring and capability to think virtuous things. He wants you to be renewing your mind (Romans 12:2). Do you believe He can make it *like new*?

c) Commit to using your mental strength for the Lord. Ask yourself, "Why do I want to have mental strength? Is it for me to enjoy life or to make my life count for the Lord and others?" Philippians 4:13 can be a declaration of your mental commitment: "I can do all things through Christ which strengtheneth me." As the Lord strengthens your mind, you can do "all things" for Him and others.

☑ What steps can you take to have mental health and mental strength in your mind?

_____

_____

2) You need courage in your mind.

When you think of courageous Christians, you probably think of their heroic deeds. Though courage is displayed from actions, it's born and bred in the mind. Courage is *"that quality of mind* which enables men to encounter danger and difficulties with firmness, or without fear."[11] Courage isn't the absence of fear; it's the firmness through it.[12]

How can you have courage in your mind? Where does it come from? Here's one answer: courage comes from what you believe.

Here's how your beliefs influence your courage:

☑ Courage comes when you believe the Lord goes wherever you go. (Joshua 1:9)

☑ Courage comes when you believe God will neither fail nor forsake you. (Deuteronomy 31:6)

☑ Courage comes when God calls you to lead and influence others to see His promises. (Deuteronomy 31:7)

☑ Courage comes from your hope in the Lord. (Psalm 31:24)

---

[11] *Noah Webster's 1828 Dictionary.*
[12] My adaptation of an original quote by Franklin D. Roosevelt.

☑ Courage comes from believing in the goodness of the Lord. (Psalm 27:13)

☑ Courage comes from God's Word. (Joshua 1:7)

Courage comes from your convictions, from things in which you are convinced. Your Christian beliefs give you more than a doctrinal statement or an identity with a Christian circle. The more confident you are in what you believe, the more courageous thinking will be in your mind!

☑ What do you believe about the Lord that gives you courage?

_____

_____

3) You need an excellent mind.

Should a Christian desire excellence? I used to struggle with the answer to this question. Excellence means to be "of great virtue or worth, exceptional, of the highest or finest quality." The word *virtue* means excellence; and the Bible encourages us to think and live with virtue.

The Virtuous Woman lived a life of excellence. Proverbs 31:29 says, "Many daughters have done virtuously, but thou excellest them all." What was part of her secret? She had an excellent mind. In order for her to do, she had to think and be. "She was in every way an excellent woman."[13]

Here are ways the Virtuous Woman's excellent mind helped produce an excellent life, a life of virtue:

An excellent mind for family: She set her family as top priority; she took care of their physical, emotional, and spiritual needs.

~Proverbs 31:11, 12, 15, 21, 23, 27-28~

Do you find setting priorities to be a continual balancing/juggling act? I know I do. Your priorities will depend on your personal family situation; an excellent option for one family may not be an excellent option for

---

[13] Charles Ryrie, Ryrie Study Bible (Chicago: Moody Publishers, 1994), p.979.

yours. Meeting your family's physical, emotional, and spiritual needs can be a challenge—especially as you go through different changes and seasons of life.

An excellent mind for your family will help you determine the Lord's best to help you set your priorities.

An excellent mind of business: She understood the real estate market to buy some land. Her on-the-side jobs include making, selling, and delivering merchandise.

~Proverbs 31: 13-14, 16-20, 24, 31~

Do you have a mind for business, but feel conflicted as to how you can use it? In your Christian circle, you might see and experience negativity towards a working woman. It can be confusing to hear accolades for the Virtuous Woman and then in the same breath to be a "keeper(s) at home" (see Titus 2:5).

Whether you work out of necessity, for supplemental income, or a desire to use your mind and gifts, here's a thought: Be mindful about you and your family's spiritual, physical, and emotional needs. You can prevent exhaustion and over commitment by simply thinking things through. Pray and ask the Lord for clarity in your mind and learn principles from God's Word to be a help with decision making.

An excellent mind for business can be a strength for your family and others.

An excellent mind to work: Her candle stayed lit at night to work on and finish up projects. Maybe she did this during the hotter seasons to rest during the afternoon heat. We Arizonans do the same during the hotter months.

~Proverbs 31: 13-20, 22, 24, 27, 30~

I'm sure your housework schedule differs from the Virtuous Woman. It's okay to not pattern your daily schedule after hers. The point of Proverbs 31 is *not* to compare your life, but to see what a virtuous life looks like. She worked when best for her, and you should work when best for you.

An excellent mind knows the best time and way to be productive at home.

☑ How does taking some time to think through and identify your priorities help your mind?

_____

_____

An excellent mind for others: She reached out her hands to the "poor" and "needy" (Proverbs 31:20); she gave them her time and resources.
~Proverbs 31:11-12, 15, 20-21, 23, 27-28~

The word *needy* really catches my eye. Reaching out to poor and needy people can be uncomfortable and draining. Have you ever reached out to a needy person but then wound up getting hurt? It has happened to me, and it also happened to Jesus. His humility of mind enabled Him to reach out to others, despite how they treated Him back (Philippians 2:5). Remember and be confident to know His mind can strengthen you. The mind of Christ gives you wisdom and capacity when reaching out to others.

An excellent mind for others discerns how to reach out and give to others.

An excellent mind to look nice: She made herself beautiful clothes from silk and purple. ~Proverbs 31: 22~

It's easy to go from one extreme to the other—from looking flashy at the wallet's expense, to looking frumpy because, "Who cares?" God's Word will help your mind to reason, think through, ask questions, and find answers: *What's my motive for how I dress? What style fits me, my lifestyle, and my ministry best? How does my dress affect my testimony for the Lord and my family?*

Dressing nicely for you may look different from the way someone else dresses nicely. I encourage you to think through and know God's best for you.

An excellent mind gives you discernment to know how your dress reflects your Christian testimony.

An excellent mind for wisdom, God's Word, and spiritual things: She spoke with wisdom and the "law of kindness," which literally means she knew the Pentateuch (the first five books of the Bible). Her fear of the Lord shows she cared about spiritual things. ~Proverbs 31:26, 30~

Do you desire to be wise, kind, and have a fear of the Lord? God's Word helps you develop each of these. All the earthly virtues in the world—strength, diligence, knowledge—become empty and vain without your spiritual life. It's your spiritual life that gives you a personal relationship with the Lord.

An excellent mind thinks biblically, wisely, and kindly. It fears the Lord and connects your spiritual life to Him.

☑ Why should every Christian lady strive to have an excellent mind?

_____

_____

I hope you can see how the Virtuous Woman's mind influenced her to living a virtuous life.

Phew! There's so much to thinking with virtue! A mind full of virtuous thinking produces a virtuous life for the Lord. May you be a virtuous woman—a woman of strength, courage, and excellence.

Chapter Nine

Thinking on Things of Praise

*Philippians 4:8: "...and if there be any **praise**,*
think on these things."

Your mind is a battlefield, a place where you fight spiritual enemies with weapons. On your battlefield, I would like you to envision another place—a secret place. This sanctuary may be a quiet clearing in the woods, a cozy fireplace in a cabin, or even a deck overlooking beautiful scenery. It's not a place you go to for relaxation or sleep. You go there to do something powerful—to praise the Lord.

Philippians 4:8 lists praise as the last item on your mindful inventory list. Praise here means "fitting for praise, something worthy to be commended of." You mind can be a place of praise—even when you're fighting a battle. When you think praiseworthy thoughts, your mind activates and influences your entire body, everything inside and out, to respond in praise.

Your mind influences your inner life—your heart, soul, and spirit—to praising the Lord.

☑ From your place of praise, your mind influences your heart.

Once you advance to your place of praise, what next? You think on things about the Lord—His Names, Word, attributes, truths, glory, reputation, testimony, characteristics, and promises.

As you think on Him, your heart—your feelings and emotions—awakens and stirs. Your heart responds to what you are thinking in your mind. Since your heart can be fickle and your feelings unreliable, it is a good thing to keep your mind in a good place to influence your heart in a good way.

David wrote in Psalm 86:11-12, "Teach me thy way, O LORD; I will walk in thy truth: unite my heart to fear thy name. I will praise thee, O Lord my God, with all my heart: and I will glorify thy name for evermore." David knew in order to unite his heart with praise, he needed to know truth.

If you want to praise the Lord with all your heart, but it feels like your praise is half-hearted, you're still in a good place. Keep thinking about the Lord, for your mind can transform half-hearted praise into whole-hearted praise. Knowing truths about God will lead you to praising Him with all your heart.

☑ From your place of praise, your mind influences your soul.

At your secret place, with your mind and heart connected, another inner part wants to join the praise party—your soul. Your soul is made up of your mind, emotions, and will (a faculty of the mind). Your soul is also a living eternal part of you. As a Christian, when you die, it's your soul that goes and lives in heaven (see Hebrews 10:39).

Your mind influences your soul because your mind makes up part of your soul. Psalm 146:1 says, "Praise ye the LORD. Praise the LORD, O my soul." It sounds easy, but what does it mean?

You praise the Lord with your soul when you combine your thoughts and passions, your mental nature and desires. It means all of your inner parts of thoughts, feelings, and passions intertwine and connect. You're not praising the Lord with your soul when you praise out of duty or obligation.

No one needs to tell you how to be *all in* for something, you just know. You have that inner "oomph." When you know you are *all in* with your praise to the Lord, that's when you know you are praising Him with your soul.

☑ From your place of praise, your mind influences your spiritual life.

Now that you are *all in* with praising the Lord, this inner part of you—your spirit—syncs your praise directly to His Spirit. God is a spiritual being who lives in a spiritual realm; your soul alone cannot connect to Him on a spiritual level. It is your spirit that connects your spiritual life to God and enables you to experience Him in a deeper way (see Romans 8:16 and First John 4:13).

For example, let's say you hear a message from the Bible that really touches and speaks to you. Your mind processes, reasons, and ponders the thoughts. Your heart swells with emotion, maybe causing you to laugh or cry. The mind and heart link to your soul, affecting your soul to stir and respond. Your spirit then expresses your entire response to God's Spirit, making it the final connection to Him.

It's both beautiful and sobering how our minds affect our spiritual life, which affects our relationship with the Lord.

☑ When should you go to a spiritual place of praise? What can you think on to praise God with all your heart, soul, and spirit?

_____

_____

Your mind influences your outward life—your physical body—to respond to praise.

Your place of praise has been a place in your mind and your inner life. Since your mind causes your body to physically praise the Lord, let's talk about where and how you can physically praise Him. The people met at sanctuaries to meet with God. Because your body is the temple of the Holy Spirit, you don't need to go to a sacred building to praise Him. Nevertheless, may I suggest you dedicate an actual place to physically praise Him? This can be small and simple, like from a chair in a room.

I used to think of outward praise as something I said and/or an occasional raising of the hands. Boy, there's definitely more to biblical praise than those two! Did you know the Old Testament contains seven different types of praise? This means when you see the English word *praise*, the Hebrew language has seven different words and meanings for it.

Your body physically responds to praiseworthy thinking by:

1) Lifting up Your Hands

~Psalm 42:5 says, "Why art thou cast down, O my soul? and why art thou disquieted in me? hope thou in God: for I shall yet *praise* him for the help of his countenance."

~*Praise* comes from the Hebrew word "yadah" and means "to use (i.e. hold out) the hand; especially to revere or worship (with extended hands)."[14]

When you are feeling pressed down, may I suggest you stop and retreat to your place—secret and/or actual—and lift up your hands to Him. Lifting up your hands signifies, "I praise You, Lord God. I'm here to worship. I surrender. I need Your comfort. I look to You. I hope in You." Like a child lifts his hands to his mother or father for a variety of reasons, the Lord draws near when you do the same. He's ready to be there to receive you!

2) Singing a New Song to Him

~Psalm 40:3 says, "And he hath put a new song in my mouth, even *praise* unto our God…"

~*Praise* comes from the Hebrew word "tehillah" and means "a hymn." This type of praise means a "new song," a song unplanned and unrehearsed. It's spontaneous praise.

"Tehilla" praise means you sing a new song once, something like a little jingle. It doesn't matter if you can or can't carry a tune. There's no need to overthink or overcomplicate this, for it is God who puts a new song

---

[14] Each of these Hebrew definitions come from *Strong's Hebrew Dictionary*.

in you. Though it may sound unconventional, I encourage you to break out in a random song about Him. You may discover you enjoy "tehilla" praise!

3) Kneeling or Bowing

~Psalm 72:18 says, "*Blessed* be the LORD God, the God of Israel, who only doeth wondrous things."

~A type of praise, *blessed* comes from the Hebrew word "barak" and means "to kneel or bow; to give reverence to God as an act of adoration." Kneeling is "to bend the legs until you rest on your knees" and bowing is "to lower your head, bend at the waist, or bend at the legs and knees."

If kneeling or bowing sounds like a physical challenge, may I suggest a simple bowing of the head? It does count as bowing before the Lord. If you can physically kneel and bow, try doing these daily. In the story about Daniel praying three times a day, Daniel 6:10 says he knelt on his knees *before* he prayed.

Let's praise before we pray!

4) Celebrating Him

~ Psalm 150:1 says, "Praise ye the LORD. Praise God in his sanctuary: praise Him in the firmament of his power."

~*Praise* comes from the Hebrew word "halal" which means "to shine, to make a show, to boast, to celebrate." It is meeting with God and celebrating His magnificence.

My family and I enjoy celebrating holidays and birthdays with different family traditions, food, and decorations. We probably celebrate them differently from the way you and your family celebrate them. Spiritually speaking, the way we celebrate God will also vary. Spiritual celebrations will differ from public places to personal, with laughter, crying, and loudness or silence. As you remember God, show He is important to you, by taking the time to celebrate Him.

5) Extend your Hand to Him in Agreement

~Psalm 50:23 says, "Whoso offereth *praise* glorifieth me..."

79

~*Praise* comes from the Hebrew word "towdah" and means "an extension of the hand, confession, sacrificing, and thanksgiving." It is thanking the Lord by showing you agree with Him, no matter what He does or allows in your life.

I'm not sure what "towdah" praise looks like, but it helps me to think of it like a handshake. To reach our hand out and accept what He gives to you. It is easy to reach out and shake His hand when you agree with Him and His plan; it is definitely not easy when you don't. "Towdah" praise thanks Him "in every thing" (I Thessalonians 5:18). Let us offer Him "towdah" praise today!

6. Singing and Playing Instruments

~Psalm 21:13 says, "Be thou exalted, LORD, in thine own strength: so will we sing and *praise* thy power."

Praise comes from the Hebrew word "zamar" and means "to touch the strings or parts of a musical instrument...accompanied by the voice; hence to celebrate in song and music." It's a combination of singing and playing instruments.

When a new song is sung a second time, it's "zamar" praise. It's listening, singing, or playing a favorite song about the Lord over and over again. "Zamar" praise can be done at home, at work, at church, and at play. However, don't let its simplicity fool you. Make sure you are intentional and listen to the message of the music with your mind, heart, soul, and spirit. "Zamar" praise focuses on the Lord and His power.

7. Loud Adoration

~Psalm 63:3 says, "Because thy lovingkindness is better than life, my lips shall *praise* thee."

~*Praise* comes from the Hebrew word "shabach" and means "to address in a loud tone, commend, praise, and triumph." It's unashamed praise, not feeling embarrassed or shy.

When David wrote Psalm 63, he lived in the wilderness of Judah. He missed going to the sanctuary and seeing the Lord's power and glory.

Thinking about the Lord's lovingkindness stirred David to his inner core. He couldn't help but belt out "shabach" praise from his lips. At first, "shabach" praise may make you feel awkward or uncomfortable. (It did for me.) Thinking about the Lord's lovingkindness will lead you to "shabach" praise.

Have you, too, been in a "praise rut"? Try applying each kind of praise to your inward and outward life. As the final inventory item listed from Philippians 4:8, praise helps you take your eyes off of yourself and place them on the Lord.

☑ Which type of praise comes naturally to you? Which makes you feel uncomfortable? Which types would you like to do on a daily basis?

_____

_____

If you have ever thought or said, "My mind's not in a good place right now," please know it does not have to stay in that dark place. At any time, you can go to your special and/or actual place of praise. A place where your mind, heart, soul, spirt, and body unite to praise the Lord of Peace and the God of Hope. A place where your battle won't seem so hard nor the enemies nearby. A place where you can draw close to the Lord, and He will draw close to you. A place where you become a woman of praise.

A Closing Prayer

Thank You, Lord, for giving to me the gift of the mind of Christ. Thank You for giving me Peace as my Guardian and the Holy Spirit as my source of grace. May I daily think on things that are true, honest, just, pure, lovely, a good report, virtuous, and praiseworthy. Please give me mental health and mental strength so I may be a testimony of You and Your power in my life. May my mind and my life give You all the glory, honor, and praise. Amen.

How to Have Peace with God

The Lord God of this entire world is a Lord and God of peace. (See the first chapter called "God's Peace" for a more in-depth study of His peace.) God lives in a place called Heaven, a place of peace. For this reason, He had to kick a disobedient angel, whom we call the devil, and his wicked forces out of Heaven.

As God created the world, He designed the earth to be a peaceful place. On the sixth and final day of creation, God made a man named Adam. God planted a beautiful garden and placed Adam in the garden to be the caregiver. God only made one garden rule—to not eat from a tree called "the tree of the knowledge of good and evil" (see Genesis 2:16-17).

Before the day ended, God created a woman from Adam and presented her to him. Falling in love at first sight, Adam married the woman and later called her Eve. Adam and Eve lived at peace with God and each other in the Garden of Eden.

However, someone is not happy about this. Someone who hates God and hates anyone at peace with Him—it is the devil. In Genesis 3, he took action and went to the garden in the form of a serpent. He deceived Eve into eating the fruit from the forbidden tree, who gave it to Adam to eat as well. Feeling ashamed, and wanting to cover up their guilt, they sewed fig leaves together to make apron coverings. They hid from God when they heard Him walking in the garden.

What happened? Sin had entered the world through their disobedience. God talked to the three of them, starting with a punishment for the serpent. God promised to one day send Someone from Eve's family tree to defeat the devil. Adam and Eve were given consequences that affect all mankind to this day.

To restore peace with Adam and Eve, God killed an innocent lamb. He made them "coats of skins, and clothed them" (Genesis 3:21). In doing so, He justified Adam and Eve. He made things right between them.

Adam's "sin entered into the world, and death by sin; and so death passed upon all men, for that all have sinned" (Romans 5:12). This death refers to a spiritual death in a terrible place called Hell (Revelation 20:10, 14-15), a place God created for the devil and his wicked forces. This explains why those who lived from Adam to Jesus Christ had to kill innocent animals and offer the blood as a sacrifice for their sins. To have peace with God. However, this only produced a temporary peace. It pictured a true peace to come.

Peace came when Jesus, as God the Son, came to earth. Born of a virgin through the power of the Holy Spirit, Jesus didn't have the curse of sin. He lived a righteous and perfect life. He "came and preached peace to us which were afar off, and to them that were nigh" (Ephesians 2:17).

Jesus willingly gave His life to die on the cross for our sins. For you! For me! He shed His innocent blood to pay the price for our sin. Jesus, God in human flesh, became our innocent sacrificial lamb to clothe us in righteousness. To make things right between us and God. Jesus "made peace through the blood of his cross, by him to reconcile all things unto himself" (Colossians 1:20).

As His dead body was buried into a grave, the devil and his kingdom evil laughed and celebrated for three days. Until something glorious happened—Jesus arose from the dead! His dead body came back to life. In triumph over death, He walked out of the tomb! His victory over death gives to all those who believe in Him victory over death—to have peace with Him.

How can you have peace with God?

♡ You admit you are a sinner. *"As it is written, There is none righteous, no, not one...For all have sinned, and come short of the glory of God" (Romans 3:10 and 23).*

♡ You understand your punishment for sin is spiritual death, and God offers to you eternal life. Romans 6:23 says, *"For the wages of sin is death; but the gift of God is eternal life through Jesus Christ our Lord."*

♡ You believe and call upon Him to be your Savior. Romans 10:9 and 13 says, *"That if thou shalt confess with thy mouth the Lord Jesus, and shalt believe in thine heart that God hath raised him from the dead, thou shalt be saved...For whosoever shall call upon the name of the Lord shall be saved."*

Look at what Romans 5:1 says happens next: "Therefore being justified by faith, *we have peace with God* through our Lord Jesus Christ" (emphasis mine).

Peace with God? Yes! My friend, peace with God is the greatest gift you will ever have. Peace with Him to live here on earth, resulting in peace to live with Him in Heaven.

♡ Have you made peace with God? _____

If you have never made peace with Him, may I suggest you do so now? There's no magical words. It's a prayer of faith, confession, belief, love, and hop

Made in USA - North Chelmsford, MA
40206_9780985989545
12.06.2023 0529